Moonika Arrak-Jaam

I Can Love You from Afar

Romantic Poetry about Distance,
Heartbreak and Unspoken Feelings

Author & Layout: Moonika Arrak-Jaam · Gemmon Publishing

ISBN: 978-9916-9201-0-7 (Paperback), 978-9916-9201-1-4 (PDF), 978-9916-9201-2-1 (ePub)

Welcome!

My name is Moonika.
Writing has been a part of my life for as long as I can
remember. I used to fill notebooks with my thoughts
and feelings, but for years they stayed only with me.

At some point I discovered that my words could also
touch others — bring comfort, awaken memories,
and tell the stories carried quietly in the heart.
That realization gave me the courage to share my
writing with the world.

If my lines reach you, I am deeply grateful. And if you
ever feel like sharing what this book has given you,
your words will mean the world to me.

Thank you for being here!

Sunset's Light

When you love, the stars shine near,
the clouds no longer seem unclear.
The sky itself feels soft and bright,
as if your hands could grasp its height.

When you love, the sun burns strong,
its warmth stays with you all day long.
No dream too distant, none too high,
for love brings wings on which to fly.

It lights the world in colors new,
and paints the grey in golden hue.
Your heart beats fast, it starts to soar,
and walking feels like flight once more.

Yes... when you love. But...

When love you give, yet none returns,
when all you offer only burns,
when longing stays, but hope is gone,
and you're the one left all alone...

When words you speak fall on deaf ears,
though you would hand them skies so clear,
When sorrow lingers, deep and wide—
then love, for you, is sunset's light.

A One Person

It's strange how one person in this world
can leave a mark that never fades
Even when years pass,
even when life carries you far away,
That person is still there—
somewhere deep inside you,
quiet, unseen, yet always present

You try to let go
You tell yourself it's the past
But then—
a voice, distant yet familiar
A fleeting glimpse from across the street
A name, printed on a page
And suddenly, it all returns

Not lost. Not forgotten

Only waiting, smoldering beneath the ash,
ready to ignite once more

I Can Love You from Afar

I can love you from afar—
from a distance, love stays light,
like a cloud so soft and pure,
drifting slow in skies so bright.

You can long for me from afar—
longing deep and dark as night,
like a storm that swiftly rises,
filling all the world with might.

Your longing aches, it pulls you under,
but love, like sunlight, finds a way,
it slips between the silver clouds
and sweeps your heavy storm away.

My love adores your aching heart,
your longing longs for love untamed.
But when we meet, our souls unite,
and love, at last, needs no more pain.

One With You

Close your eyes and let me trace
your soft, warm lips in slow embrace.
Let me kiss your trembling eyes,
like butterfly wings before they rise.

Let me run my fingers through
your silken hair, so wild, so true.
Let me feel your burning skin,
know that you are mine within.

Let me take your hands in mine,
lock our fingers, intertwine.
Hold you close, as none before,
lost in you forevermore.

To sense you breathing next to me,
to drown within your melody,
to drift in dreams within your arms,
and melt into your endless charms...

How perfect it would be.

The golden moon lights up the lake,
its glassy waves in silence break.
The trees cast shadows, long and deep,
while distant wolves their voices keep.

The restless birds call soft and low,
yet here with you, the world won't know.
Bare and boundless, free of shame,
as nature formed us, wild, untamed.

To taste, to touch, to lose control,
to claim each other, heart and soul.
So grant me this, my love—
say yes...

Close your eyes, my dearest one,
let our hearts beat as if they're one.

When I Think of You

The night is so dark,
yet when I think of you,
everything around me begins to glow...
Not a single star lights up the sky,
but when I whisper your name,
thousands begin to shine.

The clouds have hidden the moon,
yet when I recall the times we shared,
the moon emerges,
and its light brightens the night
as vividly as the sun illuminates the day.

I am not yet asleep,
but when I close my eyes,
you appear before me,
and I feel it - so good, so safe.
Because you are with me,
in my dream, every night, always...

And I drift to sleep with a smile on my face.

Make a Wish

I love the nights,
soft and secretive,
filled with unique,
slightly haunting sounds...

The moonlight reflecting
on the smooth surface of the lake,
and the trees casting shadows
on the dark earth below...

The sky adorned with shining stars—look!
One is falling.

Make a wish!

This Moment

We have no today, no tomorrow,
and none know what fate has in store.
Our truth is this moment we borrow,
together—what need we for more?

Our souls have been woven as fated,
like grain as it ripens to gold.
Above us, the clouds drift unstated,
unknowing the tales yet untold.

I don't want to leave, I would falter—
if I go, all may vanish, I'm sure.
I don't want to leave, I would falter—
this chapter may close evermore.

Winds arise and tangle our tresses,
sun peeks, but it sees us no more.
From afar, a train call impresses—
day fades as the evening draws o'er.

For a moment, I gaze in your eyes,
as a smile softly plays on my lips.
I embrace you once more as time flies,
and kiss you with love at my fingertips.

Feel It with Me

Take me, oh take me,
conquer me again.
Let me feel the warmth of your skin.

Look at me, oh look,
look at me again.
Let me feel the spark in your gaze within.

Speak to me, oh speak,
speak to me once more.
The words that make my soul so tender.

Feel it, oh feel it,
feel it with me—
This feeling that drives us both to surrender.

Do You Remember

Do you remember the day by the shore,
when we both knew—we'd meet here no more?
The sea carries ships on its vast, endless waves,
but that day, a storm through the waters raged.

We stood on the beach, just the two of us there,
as rain kept falling, drenching the air.
I clung to you tightly, like a shivering child,
while deep in my soul, the tempest ran wild.

I knew it was ending, our time had run thin,
one final embrace as I held you within.
A prayer in my heart—may love never fade,
may your soul still remember the bond that we made.

But still, our paths parted, we had to let go,
I left that place, though it pained me so.
Do you recall, my love, those bright days,
days filled with laughter, a golden haze?

Do you feel sorrow when I yearn for you?
Do you smile when I send my smile through?
Does your heart, at times, still whisper my name?
Do you dream of me too, or is it not the same?

I haven't found rest in so many nights,
each evening I lie down and turn off the lights.
I think of you, live in our moments once more,
till sleep finally finds me and closes the door.

But waking again, I ache for you still,
I open my eyes—you are never here.
Why does love ask for a price so steep?
Why must its loss cut so cruel and deep?

Time moves on, yet you stay in my heart,
I still recall the days we didn't part.
And quietly, softly, I whisper again,
if not today, then someday... but when?

Will You Ever Think of Me?

Could I ever dare to say,
"You were a friend to me one day"?
Will you ever think of me,
or am I just a fading dream?

My restless mind won't let you go,
my heart still longs—you'll never know.
For if we meet again someday,
I'll smile as if I'm okay.

Waiting in Vain

I waited for you, though I knew so well—
you would never return, no magic to quell.
I dreamed and I hoped that it couldn't be late,
though you no longer noticed me, sealed my fate.

I couldn't let go, I clung to your name,
though you had long since distanced the same.
Still, I lived in a dream where you'd one day say—
you too couldn't bear to stay away.

Yes—now I see it was me all along,
dragging the past where it didn't belong.

I'm the one who holds love in my chest,
while you closed the door and laid it to rest.
But if I live still in your memory's view,
it's enough, and I'll hold on to that too.

My eyes were shut—I refused to see,
refused to accept reality.
For sometimes my body still senses you near,
and I let myself sink in that swamp of despair.

And I wanted to stay there, waiting in vain,
to hope, to believe that you felt the same.
Yet I couldn't admit to my heart's own plea—
that I, too, would become just a forgotten memory.

But now I see that life moves ahead,
and I don't belong in the path you'll tread.
Though my heart still longs, it's time to break free,
and leave the past where it's meant to be.

If You Could See Me Now

If you could see me now,
you'd notice tiny drops
glistening on my cheeks—
painful pearls,
born from the sting
of your careless words.

If you could feel
what I feel right now,
maybe then you'd understand.
Maybe then you'd see—
a soul can ache
far worse than any wound of flesh.

But you don't care, do you?
If you did,
your every word
wouldn't shatter my heart
again
and again...

Behind the Glass

Don't be upset if I don't speak,
if I stay silent...
It's just that I have no words to say.

I sit in stillness, staring at the screen,
simply feeling you—
You, on the other side, a presence I can't touch.

Here, I can only wonder
what thoughts might linger in your mind.
I can only picture you—
sitting, standing, walking...

Your eyes, distant, looking out,
while mine, so close, still long to drown in them.

If only I could feel you again... like before.

But the screen is cold. So cold.
And there you are—
trapped behind the glass,
far from me.

Just a Little Time

Give me just a little time,
let me look into my soul.
Give me space to breathe, to find
the missing pieces of my whole.

Let me think, let me feel,
why I'm here, what path to take.
Wait—just wait—until it's real,
until I know which steps to make.

Do not ask me,
do not press, do not demand.
Just be near me,
time will weave the words unplanned.

Let me know what calls my name,
wait a moment—I beg you, stay.
At times, I hate my tangled mind,
yet you outshine all gold each day.

Give me just a little time,
let me look into my soul.
Give me space to breathe, to find
the missing pieces of my whole.

You Told Me

You told me I was dear to you,
too good, too kind, too pure, too true.
You spoke your heart,
your thoughts, your view,
with nothing left to hide or rue.

You said you'd always stay so near,
That I would always feel you here.
You told me, "I am yours, believe,"
And with you, life felt light, felt free.

You've said so much I hold inside,
and all I wished was never goodbye.
You called me precious, loved, and whole,
and I confessed—you are my soul.

You swore you'd never fade away,
but deep inside, I knew the way.
You said, "I love you," soft yet strong,
but love like ours won't last for long.

And now I sit, my thoughts run deep,
The clock ticks on, yet time won't keep.
A door creaks faint—was someone near?
Should I still hope, or let it disappear?

Who will tell me, who will know?
Should I hold on—or let you go?
Will you return, or leave me here,
drowned in silence, lost in fear?

I Need You No More

Loneliness, farewell's cold embrace,
heartache that drifts far away.
I lift my hand for one last wave,
but plead for your return? Not today.

No longer I bow before your feet—
too often I did so before.
This sorrow has torn me, made me weak,
and rules never bound us nor bore.

Your footsteps fade in echoes deep,
your shadow still lingers at night.
You need me no more,
you don't even keep
a trace of my scent in your sight.

I gaze at the void—its whisper replies:
"I need you no more—I need you no more..."

So here our roads forever part,
like echoes of dreams left behind.
I wonder, do I cross your heart?
It lasted till dawn, then declined.

Don't Come Back

Please don't come back, my dear,
you've become a stranger to me here.
Whatever we shared just yesterday,
there's nothing left for me to say.

Don't come knocking on my door,
don't beg me for a smile once more.
I'm closing this door forever tight,
do you hear me? Leave me tonight.

Go, go to where it feels right,
you cannot force what's lost to ignite.
Go—there's no reason left to stay,
I'll move on without you, my way.

Just a Plaything

You came and said you wanted me back,
that I was still dear to you.
That you'd missed me so deeply,
and couldn't live without me.

But you didn't mean it...
You only wanted to revive the feelings
that had begun to fade within me.
You wanted to toy with my heart
once more,
to make me your plaything again.

I let you back into my life,
I believed you
when you said you needed me.

I trusted you
with the feelings I held now,
I trusted you with my story...
I opened my soul to you,
I led you back to my heart
once more.

But was it all just for this?
To feel disappointment again.
To feel pain again.
To cry once more and realize
you don't feel the same.

The sharpest chords
are played on human hearts.
The saltiest tears
flow from heartbreak.

The deepest wounds
are carved by longing,
by hope, by yearning.

And the cruelest memory is left behind
when you're nothing more
than a plaything to the one you love.

Unspoken Words

I see the glow of joy still gleaming,
the light that once adorned your face,
back when you held me, lost in dreaming,
wrapped in love's unyielding grace.

Your lips would smile, your voice would tease,
each time I whispered, "I love you."
Do you recall our hopes with ease,
the path we climbed, the dreams we knew?

The endless talks, the tender hands,
the way we walked, so side by side—
each step toward the promised lands,
with love that time could not divide.

And now, at last, we've met once more,
a chance to see you, long awaited.
I longed for this, I hoped before,
yet now, my yearning has abated.

Why did you speak those fateful words?
Though soft and kind, they cut so deep.
They struck my heart like sharpened swords,
and stole the joy I longed to keep.

We stood there still, just you and I,
so close—yet kept apart by space.
No crowd to stop us, none nearby,
yet something held us in our place.

Your eyes—oh, how they longed to say
the truth your lips refused to speak.
Yet silence took your words away,
and left me longing, lost, and weak.

Maybe One Day

You may return and softly say
that you still love me, like before.
But fairy tales have lost their way—
I don't believe them anymore.

I outgrew dreams of "happily,"
the day you closed my door behind.
You left—and I withdrew in me,
to a world no paradise could find.

You may come back and hold a key,
to free me from this world of mine.
But what you bring won't set me free—
your key no longer fits in mine.

I do not trust the words you weave,
your eyes no longer pull me in.
Your hands, once warm, I cannot feel—
they touch, but don't belong to me.

I do not know you anymore,
you're just like thousands—just the same.
For all that made you shine before
has faded now into a name.

And I—I too have slipped away,
not here, not lost, but somewhere far.
Drifting in my world of grey,
untouched by who you ever are.

Maybe one day,
when I decide,
I'll let the gates within me part,
unbar the doors that hide my heart,
and step into your world again,
but not for you,
not for the love we left behind.

Maybe one day someone will come,
will lead me back to paradise,
will whisper me a brand-new tale,
one that ends in something nice.

Maybe one day I'll let them in,
but then, it won't be you who hears
my lips breathe softly, "Darling, dear."
It won't be you whose arms embrace
the fragile warmth of my new days.

It won't be you—no, nevermore—
who holds the heart I choose to give.
You threw away what once was yours,
and now, I throw away you too.

Maybe one day I'll step back out,
Beyond these walls I've built inside—
into the vast and open world,
from my small, safe world.

Eyes of Ice

I know—
one day you'll return again,
take my hand and softly plead:
"Forgive me!"

But this time,
my eyes are ice.

I Promise You

I promise you, I'll forget you in time,
I'll walk far away, leave no trace, no sign.
And one day, should you think of me then,
you won't even know how I live, where or when...

I'll tear you out from my heart so deep,
leave not a trace for time to keep.
No sign will linger, no mark remain,
to show that I once loved in vain.

I promise you, I promise this, I promise...

But please—don't watch me as I go,
don't follow as my shadow fades.
Let me vanish into the night,
lost beyond the moonlit haze.

For where I go, I leave a trail,
marked by wounds that time won't heal.
It may remind you—once we walked
a path that felt so right, so real.

So please—don't turn, don't look behind,
just let me go, set me free.
Though in my eyes, you saw yourself,
you must release and let me be.

Once We Were One

The earth grows wet beneath my tears,
for I weep for the soul of you I've lost.

Once we were one, but now we are two,
tomorrow will come, and no one can say,
if we'll find light in the day or must fade away,
to search for a beginning on the other side...

One Final Word

One final word still lingers unspoken,
my lips are heavy, my heart half-broken.
Your name still glows on the screen's dim light,
one fleeting thought: to do something right...

I whisper your name, so soft, so low,
and think of the past, the life we know.
I hope once more you'll walk this way,
I wait—and within, my heart does pray...

Then I wave goodbye, a farewell so small,
a tear dries slowly, its trace does fall.
Yet I know—your memory stays with me,
and I know—you're not so far, truly.

To the Shores of Memories

Above the hopes once vast and bright,
a mourning cloud drifts dark and cold.

The birches, bent with sorrow's weight,
bow toward the earth—scarred, cracked, and old,
and listen to the tortured ground,
where thorny roots twist, writhing deep.

The thunderstorm beats fierce and loud,
on trunks that stand in shadows steep,
while moonlight casts its ghostly hue
upon the dreams that drowned in grief.

Then suddenly—you see the truth:
the hopes once full have drained, deceased.

Your heart now splinters, cracks apart,
each fragment lost to endless night.

And all is gone—washed far away,
to shores where blackened memories lie.

A Memory to Keep

My body feels your last embrace,
your kiss still lingers, warm and sweet.
Let time not steal this cherished place,
let memories keep it pure, complete.

Now all has turned to days gone by,
yet every moment stays so clear.
You've long forgotten—but to my eye,
you'll still be precious, always dear.

No one could ever be like you,
no other holds me quite the same.
As if for me alone you grew—
yet you don't know I miss your name.

You were unique, a fleeting spark,
a flash that lived but for a breath.
So rare, so priceless in my heart—
and only now I see its depth.

Someone by Your Side

To cry,
there must be someone
with whom to share your tears that freely flow.

To laugh,
there must be someone
with whom to share the joy that makes you glow.

To heal
and push the pain away,
there must be someone there to help you through.

To feel
the bliss of happiness,
there must be someone you can share it to.

To live,
there must be a friend—
someone whose trust is steadfast, strong, and true.

No Tears for You

Tears filled my eyes, they freely fell,
when I first heard the tale you tell—
how someone else now claims your heart,
and I was left to fall apart.

You cared not for the pain I knew,
yet wished I'd beg to stay with you.
But hear me now, my voice is clear:
I'll never plead—you'll find no tear.

So go, if leaving feels so right—
without you, I'll still find my light.

A Shard of Void

I'm so weary of this gray, dull land,
this endless routine, yearning's hand,
this waiting that won't ever cease.

Now spring has come... All blooms anew.
The earth is radiant, drenched in hue.

The sun is blazing, fierce and bright.
Birds and beasts find love in flight.
People stroll, hand in hand, hearts alight.
But I— I feel alone, bereft of delight.

For me, no beauty lingers here,
no love, no laughter, hope sincere.
All that's left is barren ground,
and fists of blackened earth I've found.

My skies are cloaked in heavy cloud,
no sunlight dares to call aloud.
A frigid wind around me cries,
and flowers shun my windows' sighs.

My house decays, its walls grow mold.
the roof drips tears of rain, so cold.
My bed's collapsed, my floors give way—
their strength consumed by slow decay.

I am old— so old, so gray.
Bent beneath this load I bear each day.
My breathless soul, consumed by ache,
yearns for a beam of light to break.

With every second, I feel my chest
rend open, my heart ripped from its nest.
My thoughts explode, my mind's a storm,
my hands grow twisted, lose their form.

Until I fade,
until I cease—
no longer me,
no longer at peace.

And if one day, a trace remains—
a shred of me through loss and pain,
it will be emptiness, a silent shard,
unseen, unheard,
forgotten, marred.

I am but a shard of void…

Where to Hide the Pain

Where to hide the aching sorrow
when it no longer fits inside?
Where to let the teardrops follow
when pillows drown and screams collide?

Where to bury all the feeling
when numbness takes the place of pain?
Where to place the thoughts concealing
an empty soul that doubts remain?

Where to run? Where to hide?
Should I scream, or drift outside?
How to be? Where to go?
Should I stay, or sink below...?

What must change to make things right?
Must I turn dark or curse the light?

I weave myself into these lines,
and with my hands, these words I trace.
Perhaps you'll keep me in your mind,
perhaps you'll find in them my place...

The Abyss Calls

The ground beneath me splits in two,
the sky above weighs down my head.
Inside, I feel my breath unglue—
as if I'll fade, as if I'm dead.
Black ravens circle all around,
I stand upon the abyss wide.
Below, the demons call me down—
and here I shiver, cold inside.

The rain now lashes at my skin,
the sea foams wild, a maddened beast.
Yet still I stand, I can't give in—
is this the hour of my defeat?

Oh, help me! I still long to stay,
to see the sun rise bright once more,
to watch the waves in shining spray—
why thirst you so to spill my gore?
I'm lost enough, I stand alone,
and yes, I know—I'm not all pure.
But even those who once have wronged
still wish to live, still beg for cure.

Ah, does no soul my cries believe?
Why must my plea be lost upon the breeze?

Lost in the Shadows

Into the night fade shadows so deep,
will you vanish as well? I can't say or keep.
Unwittingly bound, your presence I've known,
what should I do with this feeling I own?

How to break free from the ache in my chest?
How to silence the thoughts that won't rest?
You're a wound that still bleeds, unhealed, ever sore,
you're the one black amidst my white's lore.

You're my shadow, my terror, my fear,
you're my fate, crushing all I hold dear.

Above me looms a sky so black,
in the distance, a lightning crack.
I long to escape this torment, this pain—
will this tale ever end? Will peace remain?
...
You will forever in brightness glow,
light surrounds you wherever you go.
But I am long lost, left far behind,
perhaps one day, a new dawn I'll find.

So Hard to Breathe

So hard to breathe on fields unchained,
where frozen earth decays in rot.
So hard to feel through dark ingrained,
a misty veil where light is not.

So hard to free yourself from all,
to walk ahead with blinded sight,
To stumble, reach, yet fear the fall—
still hoping fate will grant you light.

So hard it is, once you have tripped,
with no one there to lift you up.

Simply Gone

When one day I am no longer here,
when one day I no longer return,
you won't see my name on your screen,
you won't hear my voice when you call.

When you look at my picture
and find it faded,
when the eyes that stare back
feel distant and strange.

When you call my name
and no one answers,
when you try to remember the one
who once held you dear,
who needed you, who loved you so.

And if then, in your heart,
you feel the emptiness, the longing,
then know—
I am no longer here.
I am gone, gone far away.

Somewhere where I am at peace,
somewhere where pain cannot follow,
where longing fades,
for you will not come there just yet.

Somewhere filled with souls like mine,
with many who weep for souls like yours.

I am gone, simply—gone.

Until Fate Shuts the Door

Dark shadows linger, trailing behind,
I'm afraid to turn and see what I'll find.

You are not the one you used to be,
not who you were to me.

A black hole cries above your head,
your face—now distant, cold, like dead.

I do not know you anymore...
And so, I walk—until fate shuts the door.

The Sun Will Rise Again

When it feels like you can't go on,
when the fragile line,
where beauty ends and pain begins,
has long been crossed.

You stand still in time,
frozen, unmoving.
Nothing happens.
Nothing changes.
No one is there.

Everything around you,
everything within you,
is empty, meaningless—
grey and so dark.

You want to scream, to cry,
to tear yourself open,
to finally rest...

To rest somewhere
where pain can never find you,
where torment and emptiness,
that have devoured your soul,
would vanish without a trace.

To be away, to be free,
to be, if only for a moment—
nothing.

To feel nothing.
To know nothing.

You want to be no one.
Because sometimes,
it feels like you already are.

But know this—
there is a reason you are here.

After every darkened stripe,
the zebra wears a white.
After every longest night,
the sun will rise again.
From every sorrow,
light is born in time.

Open your eyes—
and you will see.

Unspoken Words

I know—
my thoughts feel heavy in your mind,
my actions leave you lost at sea,
and all the love I try to find
is one you cannot give to me.

I know—
for you, it's simple, clear as day,
you think I weave my pain alone,
you think my wounds, in careless play,
are cuts I carve into my own.

But still, just know—
you, too, have deeds you've left undone,
you, too, have thoughts you've never faced,
and words unspoken, lost and spun,
still echo in your heart's embrace.

Do you believe your side is right?
That all you've done, or left behind—
could never turn into regret?
Could never show what you've been blind?

Yes, I know,
I see the faults my hands have made.
Yes, I know,
much was left unsaid, unplayed.
But do you know
what lingers deep within your chest?
And do you know
where words unspoken come to rest?

Just Don't Look Into My Heart

Today, I no longer cry.
I cast the pain from my soul,
toss you out of my thoughts,
sweep away all the memories.

Today, I no longer cry!

Look at me, and you'll see—
I smile brightly at you,
laugh at all that's passed,
make fun of my own feelings,
I sing, I dance, I run and I leap.

Look at me—
today, I no longer cry...

Just don't look into my heart.
Then you will know—
everything I do, everything I say is a lie.
Then you will know—
that I still love you,
still miss you...
Always.

Unapologetically Me

I want,
I want, I want—
to scream across the snowdrifts wide,
to shout into the world's cold face,
and feel—
not all is lost inside.

I want,
I want, I want—
to call out louder than the seagulls' cries,
to know—
the ships are still moving, not yet ashore.

I want to speak,
I want to be heard,
I want to exist—fully, truly, as I am.

To be myself. Just me.

I'll Find My Way

What does it matter, where I stand,
or what I do, or where I land?
In a new form, I'll find my way,
and build tomorrow, day by day.

No matter what was left behind,
or all the dreams we failed to find.
What once we wished for never came,
what we ignored now speaks our name.

One Day, You'll Think of Me

Forgive me, but sometimes I struggle to see,
to understand all that you do.
I bear the sorrow, the ache within me,
yet part of you stays out of view.

Why do you promise, then turn away?
You know I wait—was it just words you say?
You know I cherish, I wish to be near,
yet why do I write, when my words disappear?

Am I just a toy, something fleeting and new?
Too trusting, too tender, too easy to break?
I fear what your many faces might do,
for each one may carry a hidden ache.

With each passing moment, I learn and I see,
I start to understand you more.
Yet why does it mean so little to thee,
what I think of you, what I care for?

Each time, I hope for a moment of light,
yet each time, sorrow soon follows.
Each time, I feel more lost in the night,
each time, my heart drowns in shadows.

Are women who love, who are gentle and kind,
meant only to wait for a spring that won't come?
Are they always the ones left behind,
left to wonder why love turns numb?

Why is it the fragile, the ones who are pure,
that suffer the coldest of hands?
Does no one regret when their hearts they obscure,
when warmth turns to dust where it stands?

A man knows well—she will forgive,
if only he smiles just right.
A man believes—her wounds will heal,
time mends all scars in sight.

Yes, one day, the trees will bloom,
the sun will break through skies of gray.
But will I see it? Or is my world
too used to darkness to find its way?

I longed to stand right by your side,
to laugh, to cry, to dream as two.
To believe that life had given us
a fairytale to see us through.

Though I was silent, you still knew—
perhaps too well, and so you ran.
I think you feared the depth we grew,
the closeness neither of us planned.

Life will go on, even without you,
though longing may linger awhile.
Be who you are, do what you do—
uou'll always be dear in my mind.

And if our roads must part in time,
I know—one day, you'll think of me too.

Don't Be Alone

Don't be alone when sorrow weighs you down,
when pain is heavy, pressing on your chest.
I know how bravely you endure your wounds,
but let me help—just lean on me and rest.

Allow me now to listen, hear you speak,
to stand beside you when your joy is gone.
I know that pain will never fade so quick,
yet light will find its way—it won't take long.

Life often leads through paths that twist and turn,
and sometimes all our choices seem in vain.
You may believe that no one holds you dear,
that empty hands are all you'll have to claim.

You may feel sorrow clawing at your soul,
regret and longing growing deep inside.
You crave a love that's never quite enough,
a warmth that never fully satisfies.

But know—you're not alone upon this earth,
so many hearts still cherish you and care.
And though at times your eyes may fill with tears,
the weight of love is worth the pain you bear.

There are true friends who hold you close and dear,
and strangers who would give their hand to you.
Life isn't quite as cruel as it may seem,
and happiness is not a bird that flew.

A shattered vase can still be gently mended,
a flame can burn where none believed it could.
One day, you'll smile with warmth that won't be
ended,
and find yourself in love—as you once stood.

Better to Keep My Heart

I've started to see, I understand—
it's better to keep my heart in my hand.
I longed for you, I thought, I cared,
I gave myself, I loved, I dared.

I laughed, I cried, I stayed, I ran,
but now I see—I never can.
It's better to be far from you,
no matter what my heart goes through.

So what if I thirst for the touch I once knew,
if my soul still aches, if I still crave you?
So what if my heart is tattered and torn,
beating and lost, so tired and worn?

I've started to see, I understand—
it's better to keep my heart in my hand.

I was your lover, your friend so true,
or maybe just someone to pass the time through.
Close in your arms, I was bound by your touch,
addicted to love, but I loved too much.

And still, you left me scarred and sore,
the wounds too deep to heal once more.
You carved your name inside my chest,
but left me nothing, nothing but stress.

I won't play the fool, not anymore,
I'm closing the window, I'm locking the door.
It's better I leave, it's better I run,
because now I know—we're already done.

I'm okay

Could I ever dare to say,
"You were a friend to me one day"?
Will you ever think of me,
Or am I just a fading dream?

My restless mind won't let you go,
My heart still longs—you'll never know.
For if we meet again someday,
I'll smile as if I'm okay.

Let Me Stay a Little Longer

Again, my thoughts return to you,
A restless storm inside my mind.
I cast aside what once felt true—
No fool am I, nor lost nor blind.

Yet one thought lingers, won't let go,
A picture clear from days long past.
I see your face, I always know,
Yet somehow, I still stand apart.

You are so dear, this much is true,
No wall nor distance stands in way.
You need not worry, not for me—
I only wish that I could stay.

So let me be, just for a while,
Don't close the door, don't turn away.
One day, I'll wander from this path,
But not just yet—not now, not today.

Still, let me see your name appear,
Still, let me hear your voice so kind.
Still, be with me, just for a while,
Still, grant me this—don't leave behind.

My dearest friend, my guiding light,
My laughter and my angel bright,
The one who listens, always near,
The one I trust, the one most dear.

So thank you, simply, for your presence,
For being here, for standing true.
And one soft kiss, a sweet caress,
From heart to heart, I give to you.

The Old Gramophone

An old gramophone plays a tune,
so strained, so weak,
While heavy curtains hide the light of day.
A drifting veil of smoke, like a restless vagabond,
Wanders through the room, lost in yesterday.

Please, turn on the lights.
Please, tell me you'll still be here tomorrow.
Not knowing is cruel when I close my eyes,
So light the way, don't leave me in sorrow.

Do you remember—
we swore to always be there, side by side?
You and I meant us, forevermore,
And though the road may twist and rise,
One day we'll look back at all we adore.

An old gramophone still creaks its tune,
So pull the heavy curtains aside.
Let the fading smoke linger just a little more,
Let the fire warm us deep inside.

I Love You

I sit beneath the midnight sky

Lost in thoughts of love so true,
Open-hearted, longing, still—
Veiled in dreams, yet waiting too.
Ever pure, untouched, unchained.

Yearning softly, lost in time,
Only hoping to behold—
Unforgotten, yours forever.

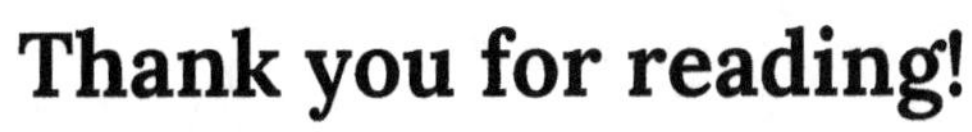

Thank you for reading!